I hope you like my book.

The Reluctant Swan

By Shirley Neff

Shirley Neff

Illustrated by Jacob Koster

Copyright © 2012 by Shirley Neff

The Reluctant Swan
by Shirley Neff
Illustrated by Jacob Koster

Printed in the United States of America

ISBN 9781624195594

All rights reserved solely by the author. The author guarantees all contents are original and do not infringe upon the legal rights of any other person or work. No part of this book may be reproduced in any form without the permission of the author. The views expressed in this book are not necessarily those of the publisher.

www.xulonpress.com

This book is dedicated to all those who love
the wonder and beauty of God's world

Acknowlegement

This story is based on true events that I witnessed at the park where I live.

Friends and neighbors watched this swan's growth and development, and we worried together as the Michigan weather grew colder and colder. "What is going to happen to our swan?"

I think we all breathed a big sigh of relief when we watched our swan actually fly away with her new companion!

What a beautiful spring day! The sun was shining brightly, the trees were budding, and the flowers were blooming. Birds were chirping and singing their songs. It was a time for new life for both plants and animals.

I was born that day on a tiny island in a small lake in Michigan.

My father was a large, handsome swan. My mother was a little smaller and very beautiful.

When I hatched from the large egg, my parents were very, very proud of me. "She is so precious!" they kept exclaiming.

Usually each spring they laid three to five eggs. My parents took turns sitting on the nest as it would be several weeks before the eggs hatched.

This time there was only me! When I was born, I was a light gray color, not white like my parents.

I was content to just stay on the island, but soon
I was gently pushed into the dark blue lake.

At first I was so scared of that water, but I quickly discovered that I wouldn't drown after all. "I can swim! I can swim!" I cried. I was SO happy!

My parents insisted that I swim betwee[n] them so they could protect me from dange[r]

My biggest enemies were the big snapping turtles who could easily grab my feet and pull me down and away. The thought of that happening terrified me, so I stayed close to my mother and father.

Then there were the geese! They loved to swim around the lake, too. If they swam on the other side of the lake, it was all right. However, if they decided to come close to us, they were in big trouble!

I still remember the day that several geese swam into our territory. My father raised up and gave some loud warning hisses. Then he flapped his wings and loudly splashed the water as he charged across the lake. Those geese flew into the air, honking in fright as they left for safer places. What an exciting sight! I laughed and cheered with glee. I thought my father was a hero.

It was a great summer. We just swam and swam. We explored the whole lake, and I loved every minute. Sometimes I was with both of my parents, and sometimes I swam with only one of them. They always kept me close so that I would be safer. Later in the summer they finally let me swim alone, but they always watched me carefully from a distance.

As the weeks went by, they taught me many things. I learned how to put my head into the lake to grab underwater plants. I learned how to go up on the land and waddle around. I learned about spotting dangerous situations and how to avoid trouble. I learned how to take care of my feathers and many other things.

My parents started to teach me how to fly. For some reason, I wasn't very interested, but I did listen to their instructions. I tried doing what they said, but I wasn't very good and didn't really like flying. I much preferred just floating on the water.

Slowly I grew bigger and began to change color. The bigger I grew, the whiter I became. It was amazing! "I look more and more like you," I said happily to my parents.

liked to swim around the lake because everything as so pretty. The trees were different shades f green. I also loved to gaze at the clouds in the lue sky, watching how they changed into different hapes. I enjoyed the cool, early hours of the day nd the setting of the sun in the evenings. What a eautiful world!

However, my happy life started to change as summer came to an end. My parents began insisting that I learn to fly better. They showed me over and over how to flap my wings, rise into the air, and soar over the water. They wanted me to get stronger and fly farther in each lesson.

I kept asking, "Why? Why would I want to fly? Why would I want to leave the water? Why would I want to go up in the sky or leave our lake? I love our lake. It's my home! don't ever want to go anyplace else!"

My parents tried and tried to convince me to fly, but I wouldn't change my mind. They talked more and more about seeing friends and relatives at near-by lakes and then all flying south together where they would be warm and safe during the winter.

However, I stubbornly wouldn't listen. "I'm staying here," I argued. They pleaded and pleaded, but I paid no attention.

Finally, with sad hearts, my mother and father flew away one fall morning. They again begged me to go with them, warned me about the cold weather, and told me that all swans go south in the fall. They told me I could come back in the spring, just like they would.

I just shook my head no and then watched them soar into the sky and leave. I didn't care. I had the whole lake to myself. I was almost fully grown and now able to take care of my own safety and food. Also, now I could just swim, swim, swim! Who needed to fly when I could just go around the lake and swim, swim, swim?

All around the lake I went. Every day I swam and swam, enjoying my beautiful home. However, slowly I began to notice differences in my world. The weather was beginning to change. The days were getting shorter, and the nights were cooler and longer. Some mornings there was frost on the ground and a little ice at the edge of the lake.

The water was getting colder, and trees were changing colors, showing leaves of orange, red, and yellow. Everything was different, but still very beautiful.

I also felt a change in myself. I began to feel alone. I still swam each day, but something was different. I missed my parents. I felt like I should be somewhere else. "Why do I feel this way?" I mumbled to myself. I finally decided that maybe I was just lonely.

Suddenly one morning I was amazed to see another swan settle into the water. He swam over beside me. He stayed around several days, and we slowly became friends. We explored the lake, and I gladly showed him some of my favorite places.

We gazed at the beautiful trees, looked at the clouds in the sky, ate the good food we found, and enjoyed just being together.

Suddenly, I was happy again! I was glad that he had come into my life. Of course I thought we would stay on this lake forever.

However, one day he suddenly announced that it was definitely time to fly south.

"Oh, no," I exclaimed. "I don't know how to fly very well. I can't fly! I know I can't do it!"

"Yes, you can," he said confidently. "I believe you can. I know you will be able to fly. You just have to believe that you can. You just have to believe in yourself. We'll fly together, and I'll be right beside you. I also promise we'll come back here in the spring. Please come with me so we can always be together."

I thought and thought about it. I was afraid to make such big changes. I was scared to have my life so different. I had been so happy here.

Suddenly, though, I knew it was time to go. It was time to fly an
not just swim. I could do it, and I would do it.

I thought of all the lessons about flying that my parents ha
tried to teach me. Then I took a deep breath, flapped my wing
hard, gave a big push, .and slowly but surely I flew into the a
and across the lake.

"I'm flying! I'm flying!" I cried joyfully. "We're heading south together. I am strong, and I can do it!

Then I gazed down at the lake and exclaimed, "See you next spring!"

CPSIA information can be obtained
at www.ICGtesting.com
Printed in the USA
LVIC041145301012
304999LV00002B